New Canaan Library

151 Main Street
New Canaan, CT 06840

(203) 594-5000
www.newcanaanlibrary.org

DEMCO

MAR 1 8 2005

Be Safe!

Stranger Danger

by Peggy Pancella

Heinemann Library
Chicago, Illinois

© 2005 Heinemann Library,
a division of Reed Elsevier Inc.
Chicago, Illinois

Customer Service 888-454-2279
Visit our website at www.heinemannlibrary.com

Designed by Heinemann Library
Page layout by Roslyn Broder
Printed and bound in China by South China Printing Co. Ltd.

09 08 07 06 05
10 9 8 7 6 5 4 3 2 1

Library of Congress Cataloging-in-Publication Data
Pancella, Peggy.
  Stranger danger / Peggy Pancella.
     p. cm. -- (Be safe!)
Includes index.
  ISBN 1-4034-4935-X (hardcover) -- ISBN 1-4034-4944-9 (pbk.)
  1. Children and strangers--Juvenile literature. [1. Safety. 2.
Strangers.] I. Title.
  HQ784.S8.P36 2004
  613.6--dc22
                                       2003024066

Acknowledgments
The author and publisher are grateful to the following for permission to reproduce copyright material:
Cover photograph by Richard Lord/Photo Edit, Inc.
pp. 4, 16, 21 Michael Newman/Photo Edit, Inc.; pp. 5, 8, 9, 10, 11, 13, 14, 20 Greg Williams/Heinemann Library; p. 6 Robert Brenner/Photo Edit, Inc.; pp. 7, 22 Myrleen Ferguson Cate/Photo Edit, Inc.; pp. 12, 18, 27, 28 David Young-Wolff/Photo Edit, Inc.; p. 15 Mark Richards/Photo Edit, Inc.; p. 17 Ronnie Kaufman/Corbis; p. 19 Rich Meyer/Corbis; pp. 23, 24, 25, 29 Robert Lifson/Heinemann Library; p. 26 Dennis MacDonald/Photo Edit, Inc.

Every effort has been made to contact copyright holders of any material reproduced in this book. Any omissions will be rectified in subsequent printings if notice is given to the publisher.

Contents

Some words are shown in bold, **like this.** You can find out what they mean by looking in the glossary.

What Is Safety?

It is important for everyone to stay safe. Being safe means keeping out of danger. It means staying away from things or people that could hurt you.

Safety is important in everything you do. One good time to be safe is when you are around people you don't know. Learning some rules about strangers can help you stay safe.

Who Is a Stranger?

Anyone you don't know is a stranger to you. Some strangers are nice. Other strangers might try to hurt you. It is not always easy to tell who is safe.

Your parents can teach you who to trust. You may meet friends, neighbors, and other people together. It is safe to meet strangers when you are with your parents.

Tricks Strangers Use

Bad strangers try to trick children into coming near. They may offer candy, gifts, or a ride somewhere. They may pretend to be hurt or need help finding a lost pet.

Never take anything a stranger offers you, even if you really want it. Never go into a stranger's house or car. It is unsafe to go anywhere with a stranger.

Do Not Talk to Strangers

Some strangers may talk to you or ask you questions. But you should not talk to people you do not know. You can **ignore** them or say "no" and step away.

It is okay to be rude or refuse to help strangers. Strangers who really need help can ask an adult. Good people will understand that you are just keeping yourself safe.

Keep Yourself Safe

Keep away from strangers to stay safe.
Do not go near strangers, even if they
are inside houses or cars. Do not let any
stranger get close enough to touch you.

If a stranger grabs you, scream to get people's attention. Fight to get free and then run! Leave your coat or backpack behind.

Be Aware

How can you know when strangers are near? The best way is to stay **alert.** Pay attention to the people who are nearby and things that are happening around you.

Bad strangers sometimes hang around
places with children, such as playgrounds,
ball fields, or public restrooms. Stay with a
trusted adult in these places. Always tell if
you notice anything strange.

Walking Safely

Before walking somewhere by yourself, plan a **route** with your parents. Practice walking it together. They can show you safe places to go if you have trouble.

Always tell your parents where you are going, and follow your route. Walk with a friend when you can. Stay **alert,** and leave if something makes you feel unsafe or **uncomfortable.**

Getting Help

If a stranger follows you or you feel unsafe, find a safe place with lots of people around, like a store or **restaurant**. Look for an adult who can help.

Police officers are very helpful people. Women with children and store workers are usually safe to ask, too. If you feel **uncomfortable** with someone, ask a different person instead.

Never Go with a Stranger

Strangers could ask you to walk or ride somewhere. They might say your parents sent them. Even if you know the person, say you want to check with your parents first.

Some families have a **secret code word.**
If your parents need to send someone for
you, they can tell the person the word.
Never go with anyone who does not know
your secret word.

Home Alone

If you are home alone, lock the doors and stay inside. Turn on lights and the radio or television to make it seem like more people are home.

Never open the door for anyone, even people you know or think you can trust. Ask them to come back later. If they do not leave, call a trusted neighbor or dial **911**.

Phone and Online Safety

When a stranger calls, do not give information about yourself or say you are alone. You can say your parents are napping or showering. A small lie is okay to stay safe.

If you go **online,** get **permission** first.
Never give anyone your whole name,
address, or phone number. Tell an adult
if people ask you **personal** questions or
if you feel **uncomfortable.**

Being Prepared

Learn your address, phone number, your last name, and your parents' names in case you ever have a problem. Know how to call your parents at work. Always carry enough money for a **pay phone** call.

Practice at home by thinking of problems that might happen. Act out how you would handle them. Practice using your **secret code word,** and learn how to call **911** in **emergencies.**

When Something Bad Happens

Always be **alert** around others. People may come too near or touch you in ways that hurt or do not feel right. They may ask you to keep bad things secret.

No matter what bad things people do, you can take care of yourself. Trust your feelings. If something does not seem right, say "no." Leave and tell an adult you trust.

Safety Tips

- A stranger is anyone you do not know.

- Never talk to strangers. Do not go places with them or take money or gifts from them, either.

- Be **alert** to who is near and what is happening around you. Tell a trusted adult if anything seems strange.

- Learn how to keep yourself safe and find help if you need it. Practice what to do so you will be prepared.

Glossary

911 phone number to dial in an emergency

alert paying attention to things around you

emergency sudden event that forces you to act quickly

ignore not pay attention

online connecting your computer to a main computer

pay phone public phone that takes money

permission letting someone do something

personal private; about a certain person

restaurant public eating place

route path you take to go somewhere

secret code word word that a family can use as a safety signal

uncomfortable feeling like something is wrong

Index